I'M NOT MY JOB

DISCOVER WORTH

BEYOND WORK

Lindsey Wopschall

TO JOE,

for teaching me the power of story and how to write my own.

CONTENTS

Part Three: Future Story

Part One:

Asking the Questions

1. WHAT DO YOU DO?

Jon didn't want to go. "But, honey, it will be good for you," he recalled his mother saying in the conversation he had with her on the phone the night before.

Jon recently moved across the country for a big job opportunity. Everything he used to do without thinking was now a challenge. He got lost driving to work. He walked every aisle of the grocery store twice before finding the peanut butter he needed. Friday night he drove straight home to sit alone, instead of going to the sports bar where he and his buddies had been meeting for the past six years.

"Just go, and if you don't like it you can leave," his mother's words echoed in his head.

Jon got into his car and pulled out his phone. He went to the recent text from his mom to find the address she sent him. He put it into his GPS. Twenty minutes later he found himself walking into an upscale restaurant.

"I am looking for the young professionals Meetup," he told the hostess. She looked down at her papers on her stand. "I have a group in the private room. It's reserved under the name Stacy. Is that your party?" she asked.

Jon didn't know whose name the Meetup event was under. At this point he didn't feel certain of anything, but he was going to give it a try. This way he could appease his mom when he next talked to her.

"Yes. Which way is it?" he asked the hostess.

She pointed to her left. Jon followed her finger which pointed

1

down a long hallway. He smiled at the girl and walked on.

As he approached the doorway, the sounds of people's chatter escalated. Then he heard laughter. It put him at ease. Maybe this wouldn't be so bad after all.

Jon stepped into the room and looked around. There were several high top tables on one side of the room. A mass of people crowded around each table. On the other side of the room he saw a bar. Only a few people stood around it. It looked less intimidating, so he walked that way.

He stood at the bar, waiting for his turn to order. He casually looked around at the other people there, hoping to make eye contact with someone to start a conversation.

"You look lost," Jon heard from across the bar.

"I guess you could say that," he replied. Jon walked over to the other young man. "I'm the new kid in town," he said acting cool and calm, hopeful of making a new friend.

"What brought you to Chicago?" the young man asked.

"My job," Jon replied.

"What do you do?" he inquired again.

As the night progressed Jon continued to introduce himself to new people. Every time a version of the same conversation transpired over and over again. Driving home from the evening he knew his mother would be happy to hear the news, but he couldn't stop thinking about one thing. Each conversation revolved around the question, "What do you do?"

Jon recognized he had uprooted himself and moved thousands of miles away for a job, but he couldn't help but think, *I am so much more than my job.*

2. MY ANSWER

What do you do? Honestly, I used to love this question because I had a very rare job. I was a TV news journalist.

"Wait. So you are like on the news? . . . Like, you are on TV? That's so cool," would be the typical excited response when people learned of my job.

Even more than the initial response I received, I loved the conversation that took place after because people were intrigued. I would be asked dozens of follow up questions about being on camera, news events, and the industry. I loved what I did, so it was natural that I enjoyed talking about it. I became the "News Lady."

My aspirations to take on a career in the broadcast industry stemmed from watching Oprah Winfrey as a child. On days when I didn't have sports practice after school, I'd come home, turn on the TV, and sit mesmerized. Oprah had an incredible ability to expose people's darkest wounds while still making them feel safe enough to share their story during her interviews. She shed light on issues that had yet to be talked about publicly on TV, and instilled a love for continuous learning as she shared how reading changed her life. I desired to make an impact on the world like she had, so I decided I would follow in her footsteps.

I knew the road wouldn't be easy to reach my dream. I knew I would face many challenges. I made my way across the country, leaving family and friends behind. I witnessed horrifying scenes covering deadly events. I experienced the not-so-glamorous side of the TV industry.

I had been the "News Lady" for three years. The realities of the news business began to get too heavy for me. I knew we all carried our own crosses. However, I could no longer see the purpose for mine.

When life gets tough I like to go for runs. Escape. Calm my mind. So one spring afternoon I found myself pacing down the Loveland Bike Trail in Cincinnati, Ohio, in deep contemplation. I was a passionate young professional who lived by the rule: If you fail to plan, plan to fail. I had it all mapped out and was on the right path. I was working my second TV news gig in a top 40 market city, a fairly impressive feat for someone early in their career in the media industry. Yet, I felt I was failing. I wasn't making the type of positive impact I knew I was meant to.

Then, in between my calming rhythmic footsteps on the trail, I heard a soft but distinct voice. "What you do will remain the same but how you will do it will change. Be open to that. Jump. The road will look foggy ahead. Have faith."

Like a wave splashing on the sand an immense feeling of peace rushed over me. I knew what I had to do.

Several days later I turned in my resignation letter at work. I had no idea what would be next. An uncomfortable place for a girl who lived her life by the motto, "If you fail to plan, plan to fail."

A few weeks later I managed to find some freelance writing and video work and also picked up a waitressing job. Despite the abrupt changes in my life I was doing well. Then one night while out with friends I was asked my favorite question. Only this time it felt more like a confrontation rather than an invitation.

"What do you do?"

For the first time I was not armed with my jaw dropping answer. I explained the work that I was doing but my audience quickly became disinterested moving the conversation to other topics.

A storm of internal questions raged. Why don't people seem excited by my stories? Did I change when I left my TV news job? Sure, I was no longer the "News Lady," but it was just a job, right?

3. THE REAL QUESTION

I have always found communication fascinating. As a broadcast major in college, I studied the subject. As a journalist I conducted hundreds of interviews and had many conversations on and off camera with people. What I have learned is that people don't always use the most accurate words to express the thoughts they are trying to communicate. Not only that, but 90 percent of communication is nonverbal! If you want to interpret what someone is trying to express you must look not only at the words used, but also understand their tone of voice and physical gestures. No wonder communication can get so confusing!

The question, "What do you do?," is a perfect example. When you meet someone for the first time you want to get to know them. You want to find out what kind of a person they are.

As I struggled with this question and my new, non-thrilling answer after leaving my TV news career, I did what I do best. I asked more questions.

While at a backyard barbecue I was introduced to a gentleman. Early in our conversation I asked him "Who are you?" instead of "What do you do?" His eyes got big, but nothing came out of his mouth.

"There is no wrong answer," I said, trying to reassure him. "I just want to know who you are." He looked around at the other people huddled around in the conversation circle. I think he suddenly empathized with the meat on the barbecue as he felt grilled by my question.

Now it's your turn. Take a few seconds and try to answer the question. Ask yourself, "Who am I?"

In conversation, "Who are you?" is a more accurate way to communicate what we are trying to ask when we say, "What do you do?" Deep in our hearts what we desire to know is what type of person someone is. What kinds of qualities they possess. Is the person standing in front of you kind, loving, trustworthy, and generous? Or are they selfish, cocky and confrontational? Finding out if someone is a CEO of a company or a bus driver won't help us discover these answers. What we want to know isn't what someone's job is, we crave to know *how* someone does their job. This is what determines who they are. Think about it. A leader can use control and demands to get people to do work or a leader can empower people with freedom and encourage innovation to inspire their organization to work. What the person is remains the same, but how they do it varies.

If we want to start getting the answers we are looking for, maybe it's time to start asking the right question.

4. CULTURE'S ANSWER

Our culture loves titles, labels, and brands. Our culture answers the question, "Who am I?" with not just our job descriptions, but also by how much money is on our paychecks and by our appearance. Do you let these things define you? What about where you live, what kind of car you drive, or the brands you wear?

The issue I have found with these answers is that they constantly change. For example; my paychecks have varied, even for doing the exact same job! My appearance has adjusted as I've matured and as my personal style has transformed over time. The possessions I have acquired fade in and out of my life as the importance to me changes.

In the 21st century we face another way our culture tries to answer the question, "Who am I?," with social media. We use things like Facebook, Twitter and Instagram to create online identities. As the author of theses profiles we are able to manipulate what other people see. We alter the images and the messages we share, carefully crafting only what we wish to show our friends on the internet. These profiles are merely snapshots of our lives, thus they cannot answer the question, "Who am I?" in its entirety. Don't be fooled or try to fool others with your social media profiles.

The truth is whenever I find myself scrolling through my newsfeed on Facebook or Instagram, rarely do I find myself filled with joy afterwards. Instead I find myself feeling left out. I see pictures of people living their lives while I sit alone peering in from the outside. Social media does not provide a person's entire story, but this is easily forgotten when we find ourselves consuming other people's meticulously curated newsfeeds. It's deceiving and harmful not only to the consumers of these profiles, but for the people who tirelessly work to maintain their manicured image.

Our culture is constantly feeding us new ways to answer the question "Who am I?" The problem is the culture is a one-size fits all solution. Our culture answers with fads, but those fade fast. Who you are is much deeper and lasts much longer than a seasonal trend.

5. FOMO

I remember the sense I felt as a teen when my cell phone buzzed. Immediately I would get the urge to answer the text message on my cell phone. Now, this anxiety has a name: FOMO, or Fear of Missing Out. FOMO is why we can't drive to work without looking at our Facebook newsfeed. FOMO is why we can't go out to dinner with friends without setting our phones on the table to check our messages in between the conversations, or even worse, during. Time once spent in silence, alone, is now spent swiping through Instagram, Twitter, and emails to ensure we are not "missing out."

The anxiety we feel when we let go of our devices stems from a need for connectivity. As humans we desire to be close. Relationships matter for our sense of well-being. However, we are looking for intimacy in all the wrong places. In an October 2012 Psychology Today article, "We All Need Some Intimacy in Our Lives," research found what mattered in predicting long-term well-being was the potential to be close with other people because intimacy increases our sense of well-being, helps us feel connected and boosts feelings of self-worth and sustain our moods. I am most fulfilled when I am actively participating in groups that interest me, like a running group, mentoring programs, and young adult groups. It's not about how many pictures I post to my newsfeed or how many text messages I get throughout the day. I feel most connected when I am engaged with the people around me with my phone tucked away in my purse. FOMO has us looking for connectivity in all the wrong places.

We feel FOMO when we see a picture of all our friends posted on our social networks. We put pressure on ourselves to be on 24-hours a day, seven days a week. But is this how God designed us?

God tells us to rest. In fact, He even rested. After He created the world, He sat back and chilled. Not because He needed the rest, but because He knew we would need it. He rested as an example for us, because the best leaders lead by example.

FOMO's pressure is real. Yet, have you ever wondered if we are getting it all wrong? As technologies designed to connect us creep deeper into our lives, we move much further away from the one relationship that matters the most, our relationship with God.

When is the last time you felt FOMO for God's connection in your life? The average young adult exchanges more than 100 text messages a day. Are you leaving room to message God? God is calling for your attention, but the more you choose to fill your quiet time aimlessly swiping on screens, the more you reject Him. The more time you spend with Him, the more you will find peace in your deepest connection.

We are so quick to turn to our culture to answer our most personal questions, but why not ask your Creator? Ask Him, "Who do you say that I am?" If you ask, God will reveal the answer to you. Will you listen?

Find a quiet place. Here God will lead you to the answers you are so desperately seeking. If you feel you need guidance, because you don't know where to start, consider reflecting upon some of these questions:

What brings you energy?

Each person has things that bring them energy and things that leave them feeling empty. I get energy when I am around people. I specifically get energy when I am around large crowds or meeting someone new. For several of my close friends, what I just described gives them anxiety and leaves them depleted of energy. All people have something that fills their tank. It's different for each person, which is why we cannot look to the culture for our answers. Again, our culture has a one size fits all solution. God made us all unique, and we all operate in different ways because of it.

What do you value?

You will spend more time and more money on things you value. I enjoy being active. I spend much of my free time running, hiking, taking cycling classes, and going to the gym. I also have spent a lot of money on race fees, boutique exercise classes, and fitness equipment. I value exercise because I appreciate what it does for my health, both physically and mentally, so I don't mind spending the time or money for these things.

What are your personal goals?

What do you want out of this life? Let yourself dream. Do you want to explore? Go travel. Do you want to run a marathon? Train. Do you want to play an instrument? Practice. Don't limit yourself to what you are doing currently. Let your imagination go. Discover what you deeply desire, then make a plan to go after it. God puts certain things on our hearts for a reason. Trust it.

The better you know the answers to these questions, the better you will have personal clarity. The more personal clarity you have, the more likely you are able to discover who you are and why you are here.

6. SIGNIFICANCE

Bruce Van Horn studied writing in college in the early 80's. It was something he had a deep passion for. While he was in college, IBM released the first personal computer. Bruce found himself fascinated by them. Using the computer he was able to edit the papers he wrote multiple times before printing out a final draft. He was obsessed! Bruce continued to gain computer knowledge and got a job on campus in one of the computer labs. The job led him to a career right out of college in computer programming. His passion for writing was put on pause, but he didn't mind. Computer programing paid him better than he could have ever imagined.

"I was on the fast track to success," Bruce said thinking back to his college days.

For years Bruce lived for, what I like to call, the chase of bigger and better. He constantly looked for ways to increase the number on his paycheck, the square footage of his home, and to fill it with more possessions.

"It's like coffee," Bruce recalled, "It never tasted as good as it smelled." Despite everything he had, he felt something was missing.

Our culture tells us success is the key to happiness. The more accomplishments you have and the more possessions you acquire, the happier you will be. Have you ever wanted something so bad you focused all your time and energy on reaching it? You think to yourself, if I just got that promotion, drove that fancy car, or traveled to that destination, then I will be fulfilled. Once you've acquired it though, just like Bruce, you realize you have a much deeper yearning that cannot be satisfied by these things.

Success isn't what our hearts desire. Think about it. Jesus was born in a city of little cultural relevance at the time. He worked as a carpenter before his ministry. He had little money and spent His time with people on the fringes of society. By culture's definition Jesus wasn't a success. He didn't acquire riches or possessions. Yet He is still one of the most prominent figures in history today. Why? Because Jesus spent His time becoming *significant* in other people's lives. He focused on touching people's hearts and souls.

When I think about the people who have impacted my life I can see that they all shared a couple things in common. These people gave me their time and attention. They coached me in conversations, giving me advice on decisions I was facing at the time. They listened to me attentively, letting me share my hardships. These people routinely showed up for me, demonstrating their dedication and care for me as an individual. They walked alongside me on my journey.

Life isn't about the things we acquire while here on earth. It's about how we interact with those around us while living. We don't get to live forever. However, the stories people tell about us can live beyond our time on earth if we make a big enough impact. Aspire to live a life of significance, not success. That's what Jesus did and today we are still talking about Him.

"We all die. The goal isn't to live forever, the goal
is to create something that will."
-Chuck Palahniuk

7. THE GREATEST STORY

As someone who has studied and worked in journalism, I see stories everywhere. Think about it. The songs you hear on the radio, the books you read, the movies you watch, even the conversations amongst your friends and family; all of these things are stories being told, and all of them follow a basic story framework.

Hero   Obstacle   Treasure

In every story there is a hero who is on a journey. During the journey the hero faces an obstacle that he or she must overcome to get to their 'happily ever after,' or what I like to call their treasure.

For more than two thousand years the greatest story continues to be told; God's story. It pulls all of us together with Truth. It's a vast piece of artwork that has shaped all of our lives. Like all stories, God's story follows the story framework.

In the beginning God gave us everything we could ever want, more than anything we could ever need. Can you imagine that? A world where every need is met and every desire fulfilled? God provided in this way when He created Adam and Eve. But then they were lured by evil and walked away from Him in the Garden of Eden when they chose to eat from the Tree of Knowledge. This is where we find the conflict, or obstacle, in God's story.

To get to the treasure, our relationship with God must be

restored. To do this God sent down his only Son who pays the ultimate sacrifice, death on the cross, for our sins to be forgiven.

This story reminds me of when I went away for college. Growing up my mom instilled in me the values and skills for the-best-way-to-live. Far from home and on my own, I had the freedom to explore and grow with new opportunities. While I explored in college I started making decisions that turned me away from her. Just like Eve, I too listened to evil whispers and made poor decisions. Each decision weakened the relationship my mom desired with me. Yet she still called me to come home, openly and lovingly. She gave me the freedom to choose when I would accept her love and teachings into my life.

This is how God loves us all. His love is given without restraint. There are no stipulations or fine print on the contract of His love. He gave us free will to make our own choices. We often fail to live under the rules He taught us, yet He continues to extend an invitation to us through His grace. He wants you, and He is waiting for you to accept His invitation.

One of the most beautiful things about God's story is that it's for all of us. In fourth grade my class was assigned to give a report on ocean animals. Each student was given a different animal. Everyone gave a presentation about their sea creature and wrote a report. Once we had all finished our presentations, my teacher had our class stand in a circle. She asked us which sea creature was the least important to the ecosystem. A few different students shouted out their answer. Then she gave me a bolt of yarn and instructed me to hold on to the start of the thread and throw the bolt of yarn to someone across the circle. She had everyone do this until each student was holding a part of the yarn. A spider like web was crafted by the yarn in the circle.

My teacher instructed me again, "Please pull on your string."

I gave the yarn a quick tug looking around the room, anticipating a reaction.

"If you felt the pull of the yarn," she told all the students, "I want you to pull the yarn this time too." Then about five people pulled their piece of the yarn together. She had us repeat this a couple more times until everyone in the room felt the pull of the yarn.

"Your sea animal might be small, like a sea urchin, or your animal might seem insignificant, however as you felt by the tug of the yarn, all animals play a role in the ocean's ecosystem. The absence of any given animal impacts the entire ecosystem. It might not be felt immediately, but all animals would feel the impact if a certain species died off. So let me ask again, which sea creature is the least important to the ocean's ecosystem?"

Like the animals in our oceans, you and I play a part in God's story. God has created you with a purpose. We all have our own story and these stories come together to craft one beautiful storyline that God has so perfectly written. All of us differ in how we were made, in our gifts and talents. Sometimes you might feel these talents are not grand enough to benefit the world, but rest assured, without you and your talents everyone else would feel the tug on the yarn.

"For just as the body is one and has many members, and all the members of the body, through many, are one body, so it is with Christ."
— 1 Corinthians 12:12

8. The Phone Call

I dialed the number. I was a little nervous. I took a deep breath sitting at my kitchen table which had transformed into my home office. I wanted to make this call a year ago, but I hesitated. Before, I wanted to call simply just to call, now I had a purpose.

"Hello! This is Bob." It was Bob Goff, the author of the best-selling book, *Love Does*. On the back of the book he had put his phone number for anyone to call. It was a radical idea, one that I admired. He sounded just as delightful when he answered the phone as he did in the stories of his book.

"Well Hi! My name is Lindsey." I started babbling. "I just quit my job. I was a TV news reporter. I love stories. I've been reflecting on the question, 'Who am I?'

"You know what you should do," Bob jumped in with excitement. "You should go to Burger King and get a job application. Bring it home. Then cross out Burger King and write God Inc. Fill out the application as if you were applying to work for God."

Our conversation continued for another ten minutes. I shared a book with Bob that I had just finished reading I thought he would enjoy. Then, we said goodbye.

I didn't go to Burger King. Instead, I immediately pulled up my resume on my computer and began to review it:

-Researched and developed daily story ideas to pitch in
   morning meetings
-Told stories live on air
-Created first social media story series

19

As I scanned my resume I realized everything on the paper was about what I did and what I had accomplished. The bullet points weren't the things I would want to boast to God about if I was applying for a job for Him. God cares more about who you are.

Working as a TV journalist in Texas I was paired to work with a photographer daily. Every day all the reporters would request to work with one particular photographer, Eddie. He had a strong work ethic, and did whatever he had to do to get his job done. Sometimes that meant missing his lunch break, coming into work early, leaving late, and sometimes doing both. Eddie was dedicated to completing his work but he also made sure that he had fun on the job. His enthusiasm and spirit made everyone want to be around him. When he received an offer at a different TV station in a bigger city, everyone in the newsroom was sad to see him leave because his presence greatly improved the office culture. Eddie was a team player. He had impacted every person in the newsroom in a positive way.

These are the qualities God wants us all to demonstrate and they are vital if we choose to work for Him. God's mission is to save each and every one of us. God desires us to work for Him to help bring redemption to the world. Working for God means we say "Yes" to being a part of the greatest story, His story. He desires us to have joyous spirits and to be diligent in our work.

God has given us all unique talents and abilities. The way we work to help Him in His mission will look a little different for each of us. We can discover our role in God's story by looking at our own story, which God has perfectly designed for each of us. Your story will reveal how God is calling you to serve. He will help you answer the question "Who am I?" more completely than answers you'll find from our culture. Our culture provides a one size fits all solution, and that solution doesn't fit our individual needs.

Our culture continues to tell us that who we are is not enough. Our culture tells us we need to arm ourselves with bigger paychecks and more possessions because our culture believes who we are is everything but our true self.

"Identity cannot be found or fabricated but emerges from within when one has the courage to let go."
— Doug Cooper

PART TWO:

DISCOVER YOUR STORY

9. YOUR STORY

We've talked about God's story and how you play a role in it. Now let's look specifically at your unique story. First, I want you to think about your life like a set of books on a shelf. These books vary physically. Some are thick with hundreds of pages, while others are no longer than a children's book. Some of these books have vibrant covers, while others are hard to notice at all. In each book there are chapters. Each chapter is made up of individual moments from your life. Some of these moments you will forget after you go to bed at night, while others will be imprinted in your memory forever.

It can be difficult to see how all of these moments thread into one cohesive story that is your life. In a 2005 Stanford commencement address Steve Jobs explained how he was able to make sense of his story. It began when he noticed higher education playing a theme. Jobs shared that his birth mother was an unwed college graduate student and that she wanted him to be adopted by people who had college degrees. He was set to be given to a lawyer and his wife, but the couple decided they wanted a girl at the last minute. Jobs was then given to a couple on an adoption waiting list. When his birth mom discovered the wife never went to college and the husband only graduated from high school, Job's birth mom refused to sign the adoption papers. Months later she signed the adoption papers, only after the pair promised they would send Jobs to college.

Jobs did go to college but, it didn't last long. He had no idea what he wanted to do with his life and how college was going to help him. The college he choose was pricey and he started feeling guilty that he was wasting the money his parents had saved their entire lives. He dropped out. Looking back, Jobs noted that it was that risky decision he made which led him to his success.

Instead of attending required classes, he started attending classes that interested him, like calligraphy. He learned typefaces and about varying the amount of space between different letter combinations. Ten years later Jobs used these principles to design the first Macintosh computer, building it with beautiful typography.

"Of course it was impossible to connect the dots looking forward when I was in college," Jobs said, "But it was very, very clear looking backwards ten years later."

To conclude the story he said, "You can't connect the dots looking forward; you can only connect them looking backward. So you have to trust that the dots will somehow connect in your future." If Jobs hadn't dropped out of college, he would have never gone into that calligraphy class which was the inspiration for the Macintosh typography.

To help identify the different books, chapters and moments, or as Jobs called them, "dots," in your life it's good to draw them out. Use the timeline on the next page.

The beginning of the time line represents your birth. The right end is this present moment. Take some time to write down ten (or more if you can) memorable events in your life. Map these events in chronological order on the timeline.

You might begin to notice that some of your events in your life were negative experiences, while others had a very positive outcome. To differentiate the two types of events, write the experiences that were positive above the timeline and the negative ones below it. Later we will go into more detail to address how God uses these negative events in our lives.

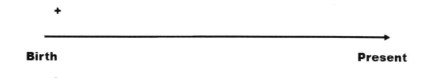

Birth   **Present**

Questions to consider while selecting moments for your timeline:

- When did you experience transition?

- When did you achieve a major accomplishment?

- When did you come to a crossroad in your life and have to make a choice?

- When did the actions of others hurt you?

- When have you experienced loss?

- When were you overwhelmed with joy?

10. PERSONAL PURPOSE

February 1st, 2001. I remember that day the same way most people remember September 11th; Crystal clear. I was ten-years-old. I was sitting in the TV room on the couch nestled tightly in one of the corners. The cushion was worn in. We really should have rotated those cushions since this was the place where everybody would watch TV, but we never did.

Whenever my dad would lay on the couch watching TV I would sit in this very spot. He would naturally bend his legs at a ninety-degree angle creating a small nest like space between his legs and the back of the couch. I would happily snuggle in. It wasn't as cozy without him there.

That night as I sat curled up on the couch, our door never shut as people came in and out of our home. As they walked inside they made their way to the back of the house, to my parent's bedroom. There my father rested. He'd been battling cancer for over a year. When he was first diagnosed doctors told my family he was untreatable, that he would die the next day. He had a rare cancer in his bile duct. There had only been two thousand cases of it in the United States.

My dad was a fighter. He got through most of his pain because of his positive attitude and sense of humor. He was the type of guy that could never be serious. Growing up, I recall my mom slicing up watermelon in the summer to accompany our dinner. Then my dad would remind us all not to eat the seeds. "If you eat the seeds you'll get watermelons growing out of your ears. Just like little earrings."

He then casually caressed his ears, demonstrating to my sister and I what these watermelon earrings would look like. "How do you know?" my sister would ask in disbelief. "Because it happened to me," he would say with his signature-crooked smile. "Oh yeah. I ate those seeds and watermelons grew out of my ears so fast! Big ripe ones. My mother had to take her gardening trimmers and cut those vines right out of my ears," he explained.

My sister and I believed him. . . the first time at least. Eventually we realized it was a fib and got tired of hearing the same old joke over and over. What I didn't know then is how much I would long to hear him say that silly old joke just one more time.

Still sitting firmly planted on the couch, I stared at the TV. *Zenon*, the Disney Channel Original Movie, was playing. I began to hear my grandpa's slow footsteps coming down the hallway. Each step he took brought me closer to the harsh reality I was about to face. When he reached the den he walked up to the side of the couch and knelt down on one knee. He looked into my eyes while mine remained on Zenon's search for Protozoa.

"He's gone," he said to me as a tear rolled down his face.

I didn't flinch. Not a muscle moved in my body. After a few moments of silence and seeing my reaction, or lack of, my grandpa gently got up and retreated back to my parent's bedroom. Not a tear left my eyes that night, and they didn't for many years to come.

●●●

When I think about my story, I always go back to that night on February 1st. I lost one of the most important people in a child's life, but from it I gained an understanding of life; its beauty and its fragility. A deep desire was planted in me to share with people how precious life is. It was this moment that led me to want to share my experience, like Oprah had, and help others with their own. It's my purpose.

If you look back on your timeline you will also discover a moment in your life which reveals your purpose. Maybe you experienced it as a child or maybe you had the moment just yesterday. Everybody has this moment. I know a woman who was married raising children when her husband got into a severe car accident, paralyzing him. It was then she realized her purpose was to aid people through rehabilitation. She became a nurse.

Don't be fooled. Your moment of purpose doesn't need to be a traumatic event. It could even be a simple conversation. Something that, initially didn't seem significant. But looking back to connect the dots, you can easily identify it was that moment which led you to where you are today.

Once you discover your purpose many of life's big questions will become clear to you. You will know with certainty who the important people are in your life. You will know how you want to spend your time. You will not get distracted by small worries and fears because you will have a clear vision of your priorities.

Ultimately, knowing the answers to these big questions will help you navigate the smaller decisions you have to make daily. The answers to those big questions become a filter for you to say a powerful yes to the things that matter most and to say a firm no to the things that are less deserving of you attention. Discover your purpose, then pursue it with passion. When you do you will see how God is unfolding your journey for you one step at a time.

"For I know the plans I have for you, says the Lord, plans for welfare and not for evil, to give you a future and a hope."
— Jeremiah 29:11

11. SHAPE YOUR STORY

In fourth grade my class did popcorn readings. Each student took turns reading out loud a different paragraph of a book. This always made me nervous. I stumbled through words often and never wanted to do so in front of all my friends. Instead of listening to my classmates as they read their paragraph, I would count the number of people ahead of me to find out what paragraph I was going to read. Quietly to myself, I'd read through the words over and over again.

When my turn came I slowly read the paragraph, sounding out the words as I went. Despite my previous practice, I'd fumble over the words. One afternoon, during this reading exercise a classmate shouted over my faltering voice, "Lindsey, you don't know how to read!"

There was some truth to what that boy said. Reading was not my strongest subject. I had been struggling with it for years. In kindergarten I had been diagnosed with Dyslexia and began tutoring to help me cope. I practiced writing words in salt to feel the words being made. I traced the shape of the word to help memorize what each word looked like. No matter how much I practiced though, it felt like a constant game of tag as I would try to chase after all my classmates reading ability, only I'd never be able to catch up.

The worst was Friday mornings, when we would have our spelling tests. Leading up to the exam I would study with my mom. I would practice spelling the words dozens of times at our kitchen table as she made dinner. I spent time preparing, yet I would never be able to achieve a perfect score. After taking the test all my classmates would chatter about their scores. Many would express how they had forgotten about the exam altogether and were able to spell every word without error.

Later when my mom picked me up from school she'd ask how I did. I would explain my normal frustrations of missing a few words then tell her how everyone else didn't have to study but still did better than I had. "Determination and hard work will pay off in the long run," she would always tell me.

I was constantly agitated. Every week the same thing would transpire, but rather than letting the kid's chatter consume me, I chose to listen to my mom. Each Friday I echoed her words in my head, "Hard work and determination pay off," and I trusted one-day mine would.

It's common for people to refer to these experiences in our lives as "defining moments." This is a problem. When you let moments, experiences, or roles that you play in your life define you, you are essentially saying these things are your identity. They become your answer to the question "Who am I?" But what would happen if you define yourself as an athlete and then get into a car accident and you become paralyzed? What if you define yourself as the CEO of a major company only to get fired? With these losses would also come the loss of your identity.

No one thing will define you in your journey. Moments like the one I experienced in the classroom, struggling to keep up with the other kids, are *shaping moments*. You cannot control every aspect of your life but you can control your effort and attitude. Your effort and attitude can help shape your story. Most often we remember the tone, the emotions, and feelings we experienced much more than we remember the specific events of our story. You have the power to influence these elements. Influence wisely.

Instead of listening to the snarky comments of my classmate I chose to listen to my mom. Instead of seeing each letter grade I received in school as a failure, I saw it as a challenge to do better next time. Tough times are going to happen in your life, but how you choose to move past them is up to you.

"When we deny the story, it defines us. When we own the story, we can write a brave new ending."– Brené Brown

12. FACING DARKNESS

If you ask me where I am from, I will proudly say Pasadena, California. It's the home of the Rose Bowl, "the granddaddy of them all." Accompanying the college bowl game is a tradition that has been held in Pasadena for more than 125 years: the Tournament of Roses Parade. For thirty of those years my dad was a member of the tournament group. Some of the best memories I have of my dad revolve around the days and weeks leading up to the New Year's Day Parade.

The parade is full of florally decorated floats, horses, bands and yes, a queen and court. It's a big deal in Pasadena. Every fall about 1,000 high school senior girls apply to be one of the seven girls in the court who make their way down Colorado Boulevard on the day of the parade. Leading up to New Year's Day the court attends about 200 social engagements and service activities. Macy's gives the girls a new wardrobe and they receive a full makeover. Sounds like every high school girl's dream, right? It was mine, but my motivation was different.

The Tournament of Roses wasn't just something my dad did, I believed it was part of who he was. My family even had his memorial service at the Tournament of Roses House after he passed. As I grew up I realized time was not on my side, because the older I got the further I was from the memories I had with my dad. I yearned to make more.

My solution? Become a part of the Tournament of Roses queen and court. It may sound silly, but my high school self was convinced that if I were to make this court I would somehow be able to reconnect with my dad by becoming a part of something he loved. Essentially this would allow me to write a new chapter of my life with him, create another memory, regardless of whether he was alive or not. So I set out for the win. I began preparing a year out.

To help me win the crown, what better way than to apply all the lessons I learned from the book I had just read called, *The Secret*. If you haven't heard of this book, essentially it describes the power of positive thinking. If you think it, believe in it, and focus on it long and hard enough your dream will become a reality. I was 100 percent bought in. Nine months before the tryouts for the court, a crown was drawn with a white board marker on my bathroom mirror. As I did my morning routine, the crown sat perfectly placed atop of my head. A single rose was scribbled beside it. Every night before I would go to bed I would visualize the letter of acceptance arriving in the mailbox. The text was Times New Roman, addressed to my name. The upper left hand corner had the Tournament of Roses logo on it: the simple stenciled red rose with its two green leaves.

My fall semester of senior year approached quickly which meant tryouts for the court began. The first tryout consisted of the 1,000 plus girls walking down a red carpet. We each had 20 seconds to greet the judges, state our number and why we wanted to be a part of the Tournament of Rose's court. Afterwards, 250 call back letters were sent. As if I was pulling it out of my dreams, I received one of the letters. Again I went back for my tryout wearing my mom's old red dress and pearls. In this interview you stood individually in front of the judges and were asked a series of questions. I remember faltering on one, letting my nerves get the best of me.

"Let me start that one over again," I said.

I collected myself and pressed on. I remember spiraling down with doubt thinking this is over. My mind focused now on the mistake. If you know the book *The Secret*, then you know that it takes time for the universe to align with your thoughts. Cut 75. I made it, despite my negativity. The red rose in the corner with Times New Roman font appeared in my mailbox again. Now I had another chance to make not just the court but the connection to my dad I longed for.

Then, cut 25 came. This was the last cut before they picked the final seven girls.

I knew the letter was to come in the mail that Monday but it didn't show. My mom tried to calm me down… "No, no, hun, I think it will be here tomorrow." I didn't have to wait until tomorrow's mail to confirm what I already knew. When I got to school that morning I discovered another girl who was still in the running had received her letter.

Emotions I didn't even know I possessed welled up inside me. I grabbed my stuff and marched out of the school cafeteria. The tears that were absent the day my dad died were now uncontrollably plunging down my face. I went straight home and found myself beating my head against our long hallway wall. Each bash to my skull echoing louder just as my grandfather's footsteps had when he came to tell me my dad had passed. I had snapped. All I wanted was to physically feel the pain that ate inside me.

❋❋❋

When my dad passed away many condolences came, for which I am grateful. One of those messages, however, still irks me: "Time heals all."

Time never stopped me from wanting to hear my dad yell for me in the stands when I made the clutch double play in my softball game at second base in high school. Time didn't stop me from wanting to hear my dad tell me I was beautiful before my date picked me up for my senior prom. I missed my dad on my college graduation day and I'll miss him when he's not there to walk me down the aisle. When you experience something difficult in life, like losing a loved one, it's like getting a really bad cut. Sure your skin grows back, but you are left with a mark. We call these marks scars. I was scarred when I lost my dad. It will forever be apart of me and my story, just like the scaring circumstances you have experienced on your journey. On the surface scars appear as imperfections on our bodies. However, scars are the physical prints of our stories that mold us and make us who we are. Our stories are our truth, and nothing is more beautiful than truth.

"We know that in everything God works for good with those who love him, who are called according to his purpose." – Romans 8:28

13. REDEMPTION

When I discovered I had lost my chance to become one of the Tournament of Roses queen and court members, a family friend came to me.

"Experiences like this build character," she said lovingly.

"Character?" I later questioned to my mom dramatically. "I think I have enough character. My cup is *overflowing*!" At the time I was a very spunky teenager. I was unable to accept our friend's statement and unwilling to take a second look at the experience I was facing because of the anger and pain I was feeling.

Recall earlier I showed you the framework for every great story. Every story has a hero, an obstacle and a treasure. Every character in a story will face an obstacle, just as you face obstacles in your life.

The word "redemption" is rooted in the Latin word, *redimere*, meaning "to regain." Amidst our biggest obstacles we all have the opportunity to find something good. It can be a life lesson, a new perspective or perhaps a new friend you meet along the way.

For many years I struggled to find any redeeming qualities from my experience of trying out for the Tournament of Roses queen and court. Why wouldn't God give me this experience? I had already lost my dad; why couldn't I have the chance to grow closer to my father?

Many years later I found myself reading Sheldon Vanauken's, *Severe Mercy*. In the book I discovered the concept of a second death. Essentially a second death is an experience someone needs to go through to let go of someone who has passed away.

When my dad passed away I didn't allow myself to go through a meaningful grieving process. I didn't shed any tears, and rarely would I get emotional talking about his death or the pain I went through. At the time I believed tears were a sign of weakness and I was not willing to be weak. I boxed up all of the pain and agony I felt to continue on in my life. Now I have learned that feelings buried alive never die.

The experience I had through the Tournament of Roses tryout process gave me the opportunity to properly grieve. I confronted the reality in my life; that I would not be able to create more memories with my dad because he was physically gone. It's what I lost; a future with my father. This second death experience forced me to open the feelings I had locked away for so long and had me embracing their intensity. Time didn't heal, but it gave me the opportunity to go through the darkness I was avoiding.

While working as a reporter people would often ask me, "What's your favorite story you've covered?" I am not one for favorites, but I would ring off several stories that personally inspired me. For example, there was the family who had lost their two-year-old son in a boating accident because he wasn't wearing a life jacket. It was a tragedy. However, from it the family started a foundation to help educate others on the importance of boat safety. Another family started a blood drive in memory of their daughter who died hours after she was bitten by a rattlesnake. It was donated blood that allowed the young girl the time necessary for her to say her goodbyes to her loved ones. A high school girl diagnosed with cancer inspired her community and classmates to live life with passion and zest despite her odds of surviving.

All of these stories are stories of redemption. Each person demonstrated that even in the negative turns of our lives we are able to make positive change and find meaning in them.

These people made a choice. They chose to find redemption and do something about their situations. When we face trials in our lives there is a temptation for us to choose to be victims. Recall how I responded to my family friend's comment… "I have enough character."

The story framework is broken down into hero, obstacle, treasure. It is not victim, obstacle, treasure. Victims are powerless. God designs heroes. He desires you to be the hero of your story. He has provided you with the tools to empower you to be a hero and overcome the tragedies you face and to discover the redeeming aspects in them, just as all the people did in the stories I reported on.

God wants you to work for Him. He is preparing you to serve through your story. He does this with both the positive and the negative experiences in your life. Take a moment to go back to the timeline you created of your life. On the timeline notice the negative events. To find healing in these negative events it is our job to discover the deeper reason behind these moments of suffering. It requires us to find redemption.

People who choose to be followers of God are tested, sometimes to even more extensive lengths than those who walk away from God. After Mary said yes to God's call she faced many obstacles. When she came to her fiancé, Joseph, to tell him the news of her pregnancy, his first reaction was to call off the wedding. Society shamed her for her unwedded pregnancy. She endured these challenges and maintained her faithfulness to God's call. By doing so she gave birth to Jesus.

What experiences do you need to revisit in your life to find redemption? Go back to the negative points on your timeline. The most incredible aspect of redemption is that once we find it, we also uncover liberation in our sufferings.

"Don't sidestep suffering. You have to go through it to get where you're going."
— *Katherine Ann Porter*

14. LIFE'S MOMENTS

Currently I work as a consultant helping businesses and leaders develop and grow. When I talk to leaders about employee engagement I always talk about the different moments an employee experiences. If leading effectively, managers will steward these moments for their employees so that they experience them in a meaningful way. We break these moments down into four types; Change, Milestone, Learning, and Every Day.

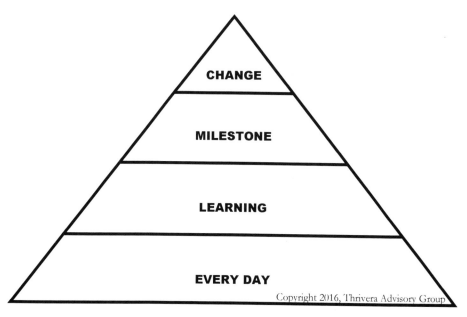

Copyright 2016, Thrivera Advisory Group

Similarly we also experience these four types of moments in our spiritual lives.

I have always been someone who writes. It's helped me to process what is happening around me. The first time I started scribbling down my thoughts was the night my dad passed away. I remember grabbing one of my dad's yellow legal pads trying to capture the moment in words to make sense of it all. Throughout my life I have continued this practice and its developed into a daily habit. It's my quiet time, my time of reflection, my Spiritual Every Day Moment.

What is difficult about Learning and Every Day Moments is that they require more intentionality from ourselves. If we want to have a deep personal relationship with God, we need to make time for Him in our lives. Are you finding ways to incorporate God into your day to day? Do you seek opportunities to learn and grow through retreats, reading good spiritual books or connecting with mentors for spiritual direction?

It's easy to dismiss Learning and Every Day Moments because they are lower on the pyramid. They don't seem as important as the Milestone and Change Moments. It's this mentality that puts you in an unfulfilled place in your spiritual life. Every Day and Learning Moments are the foundation. These types of moments might not garner as much praise or recognition. Often they are done in private. However, Every Day and Learning Moments are the foundation. Without the consistency of these moments in your life you will be unable to experience your Change and Milestone Moments in a meaningful way.

All these moments are the moments that shape your story These moments have the power to influence your journey a great deal. Knowing this, how do you wish to prepare for these moments in your life?

"Life isn't a matter of milestones, but of moments."
— Rose Kennedy

PART THREE:

FUTURE STORY

15. BECOME

We all have dreams and aspirations. God places these on our hearts. These desires inform the decisions we make to create our future story.

While speaking to a Sunday School class full of fifth graders one morning I started asking them about their lives.

"How many of you play sports?" I asked.

Half of the students eagerly raised their hands.

"If you want to be the best at your sport, the best soccer player, the best runner or the best golfer, what do you have to do?"

"Practice!" one student shouted out. "I practice each week to prepare for my games on Saturday."

Then, I wrote this word on the whiteboard.

Become

If you want to become something great, like a great athlete, you must... I crossed out half of the word.

Be ~~come~~

You must presently be the athlete you want to become in the future. Now is your time. Practice. Not yesterday, not tomorrow. This moment. Right now. You must be who you want to become. This is how you will seize the dreams God has placed on your heart.

Archbishop Fulton J. Sheen said, "If you don't behave as you believe, you will end by believing as you behave." We are the writers of our own narratives. What we tell ourselves we become.

You can be your own worst enemy or your biggest cheerleader; it all depends on what you choose to tell yourself. What are you telling yourself? Like a boomerang, whatever you put in the world will come back to you. If you are a grouch who struggles to find good, your life will be one full of bad days and unhappiness. If you choose to see beauty, you will find endless breath taking moments throughout your life.

Many of us are familiar with the Bible verse, "Ask, and it will be given to you; seek, and you will find; knock, and it will be opened for you," in Matthew 7:7. It's good practice to ask ourselves, what are we asking for? What are we seeking? Do you choose to acknowledge the misfortunes in your life? Do you count how many times you were cut off on your way to work or, do you choose to find the ways in which your co-workers have been helpful to you throughout your day?

Your reality is all about perspective. If you perceive a world where acts of kindness are acknowledged, then your reality will be one where kindness is present. It all starts with you and what you are asking and seeking for.

Do you know who you want to become? The initial decision is the easiest. For example, everyone says they want to be healthy. But, it's hard to choose an apple over a cookie each and every day for lunch. It's hard to get up when you hear the sound of your alarm clock for a 5:30 a.m. workout. The more clear your vision of who you want to become is, the less difficult these daily decisions will be for you. The decisions you make craft your story; the journey you are on, the journey to who you will become.

"You are what you believe yourself to be."
— Paulo Coelho

16. WANDERLUST

When I travel to new places I get giddy with a childlike wonder because everything I experience excites me. When is the last time you went to a never-before-seen place? What was it like? Were you nervous, scared, or excited before you went? What about while you were traveling? What did you feel?

When I think back to all the different trips I have taken throughout my life I recall vivid memories. Heck, I remember my family vacation in Hawaii when I was six-years-old. I remember swimming with dolphins, getting a cut on my ankle from walking on volcanic rocks and receiving a pin with wings from our pilot when my family was flying home. I remember aspects of this trip from 20 years ago better than I can remember what happened to me last Tuesday.

When we travel our senses are heightened. We pay attention. We look at people as they pass by. We taste the flavors in what we eat and drink more vividly. We notice the architecture of buildings and the landscape of our surroundings. We allow time to take in the moment. It's no surprise then, why the term wanderlust has become so popular. We leave our stuff at home, and travel with only the essentials because when we travel we know stuff isn't going to make our journey any more meaningful. In fact, the larger the pack you carry on your journey the more you will be weighed down.

So let me ask you, why do we limit ourselves? Who says you can only experience life with your senses fully turned on when you travel? No one. But we get lazy. We get caught up in our routines and numb ourselves to what's around us.

While working as a local news reporter, I always felt it was my obligation to know the community. How could I tell stories about people and places if I didn't fully grasp the culture and know the local history. So I did research. I invested time in getting to know the community. I wouldn't just read about the cities; I would explore. One friend would always have me drive wherever we went because she said, "Lindsey, you know all the roads," despite her growing up in the city her whole life and I only being a recent resident. In the small Texas town it was common to hear, "There is nothing to do in this city." When I heard this, I would often respond with a brief list of the different organizations I was active in, people were amazed, "I had no idea," they'd say. Just because you aren't traveling, doesn't mean you should stop exploring.

It's commonly believed we must have these grand experiences to fully appreciate life. You must go skydiving, climb the highest peaks, and travel to distant countries. However, if you live with your eyes wide open, you will discover beauty in the everyday. You'll find joy watching children play in the fall leaves and see beauty when the flowers sprout in spring. You will learn to take in each moment no matter what part of your story you are living. You will see there are people in your own neighborhood who need your ministry. Wanderlust doesn't require you to have dozens of stamps on a passport. It requires you to live in a way in which you are fully open to the journey God has set before you.

"Holy Spirit, may my heart be opened to the word of God, may my heart be open to good, may my heart be open to the beauty of every day."
- Pope Francis

17. MENTOR

Rooted deep in America's culture is the idea that if you work hard enough you will achieve your dreams. If you put in the extra time you are deserving of the riches that will come to you. It's America's promise.

Pharrell Williams is a Grammy-winning producer, songwriter, and artist behind some of today's most popular R&B, rap and pop hits. I remember watching the April 13, 2014 episode of CBS Sunday Morning. In an interview he was asked about his accomplishments, how did he do it all? His answer didn't follow the American Dream.

"My story is the average story, it was just filled with special people," he said.

In the interview the reporter challenges Pharrell, "You are giving everybody else credit."

"Well, what am I without them?," Pharrell retorted, putting the emphasis on the people scattered throughout his story that helped guide him to where he is today.

So often I take credit for my achievement. I'm prideful. I like to share a story that reflects the American Dream. I recall the summer after my freshman year of college. I took two summer school courses, worked two jobs and taught swim lessons in my backyard. I remember how I fought for the opportunity for an internship at a local news station, calling over and over again, doing everything I could to have the experience.

Pharrell sees the bigger picture. It's true he put in the long hours, but God who created him, gave him the strength and talent. God put people like Pharrell's band teacher in his life to instruct him. It's the perfect combination of grace and works.

When I spend time reflecting on this, my pride is replaced with gratitude. For I see that it wasn't what I did, but it was the opportunities I was given and the people that coached me along my journey.

In all great stories there are mentors helping to guide the hero. In the Disney classic *Cinderella*, the Fairy Godmother helps Cinderella when she finds herself at her lowest point, stuck at home unable to attend the prince's royal ball. She helps to give Cinderella comfort, strength and belief in herself. In Star Wars, Obi-Wan Kenobi gives guidance to Luke Skywalker. Obi-Wan Kenobi even passes Luke's father's lightsaber down to him.

You too, have mentors in the epic journey God created for you. They can be a parent, grandparent, friend, coach, or teacher. Some mentors walk with us for only a few chapters of our lives, while others stay with us throughout our entire journey. God is our greatest mentor, are you using Him as a resource? How would your story change if you intentionally went to God when you were in need of some advice?

Spend some time listing the people in your life who have helped you on your journey. Think about what gifts they gave to you or lessons they taught you.

Mentor   **Lesson Learned**

_____   _____

_____   _____

_____   _____

_____   _____

_____   _____

18. SURROUND YOURSELF WITH GREATNESS

U.S. Olympic swimmer Ryan Lochte is a well decorated athlete. He has competed in the Olympic games in Athens, Beijing, London and Rio de Janeiro. Within those four Olympic games he has racked up a total of 12 Olympic medals: six gold, three silver and three bronze. Lochte has demonstrated what determination and dedication look like as an athlete. However, it's easy to overlook his accomplishments when you put him beside his competition.

Michael Phelps holds more gold medals than any other person in the world. He left the Rio Olympics with a career count of 23 gold, three silver and two bronze medals, and I'd imagine a sore neck from carrying around all that bling.

The two U.S. swimmers have had a tense rivalry in the pool for 13 years, with Lochte most commonly trailing behind Phelps. You'd think Lochte would be bitter, jealous and frustrated for not being able to have the career accomplishments that Phelps' holds. However, Lochte's rationale is much different.

"I wouldn't be the swimmer I am today if I didn't have Michael," he said. "We both push each other and bring the best out of each other," Lochte said during an ESPN interview at the U.S. Olympic trials in Omaha, Nebraska in 2016.

Lochte truly believes had it not been for Phelps, he wouldn't have achieved the 12 medals and two world records he holds. Phelps could be characterized as Lochte's enemy, but Lochte believes Phelps is a main driver for his success.

We tend to shy away from putting ourselves in groups of people who are better than us out of intimidation. Like Lochte, maybe your accomplishments don't look as admirable when you stand next to the best in the business. However, you must realize the real race isn't against the people around you, but the person you were yesterday. The people around you are only meant to propel you forward. The story God created for you is for you, and you alone. The goal is to become your best self. We do this by improving each day. It's not about becoming better than your competition or in Lochte's case, better than Michael Phelps.

If you want to craft a great story, you need to surround yourself with people that will push you. This means putting people in your life who work hard towards their purpose and inspire others to do the same. It's true you become the average of the five people you spend your time with.

The first time I intentionally implemented this concept into my life was when I focused on becoming my best self. I was adamant about only spending time with people who were joyful, fulfilled in their work, and hungry for continuous learning. I found myself intrigued with how these people spent their time, what books they read, how they worked, what they would eat, and their exercise routines. I put myself amongst people who were doing things better than I could. For exercise, I ran with faster people. For business, I sat with people who had built their own companies from scratch. For wisdom, I learned from people who had years of life experience. In return, I became faster, more savvy in business, and wiser. What do you want to become? Find an expert and learn from them.

"Surround yourself with only people who are going to lift you higher, life is already filled with those who want to bring you down."
— Oprah Winfrey

19. THE STRUGGLE IS REAL

A young boy growing up in East Los Angeles in the 1960s was raised by his mother's strict philosophy, "Move forward. Do the best you can with what you have and never give up." The boy and his family didn't have much at all, which inspired the young boy to get creative. When his shoes became too worn, he learned that if he cut out a piece of cardboard and placed it under the insole of his shoes, he could get more wear out of them. When he got a hole in his pants he would take an iron on patch, iron it on to cover the hole, then sew over the patch to reinforce it. Everything in his life was a struggle, but with his mom's words in mind he persevered.

With a passion for sports, the boy made his way to the University of Southern California playing both baseball and football. His career on the football field was minimal due to persistent injuries. As a freshman he tore a ligament in his right knee, and as a junior he tore another right knee ligament. Then, during his senior opening game in Lubbock, Texas, he felt like he had been shot in his left knee, a pain he was very familiar with.

Lying in the hospital bed after the third knee surgery of his career a reporter asked, "When is enough, enough?" The boy replied saying that God had given him the passion to play and he would not quit. He dug deep and focused on recovery. During the next three months, he centered his life around his school work, attending classes, rehabbing his knee and working out. After each day he'd go home to his one-bedroom apartment and used his wife's shoulder to cry on. His journey was filled with pain. Physically and emotionally.

He went to his head coach requesting to play in the college bowl game. His coach was hesitant, concerned for the boy's long term health. However, he told him if the doctor would clear him to play, he would.

January 1st, 1980, at the Rosebowl, "the Granddaddy of them all," the boy heard his name called out in the starting roster. He played the entire game, including the final 85-yard game winning drive. Months later he received a call.

He whispered excitedly to his wife, "it's the Bengals." He was chosen third in the first round of the NFL draft. He moved with his wife to Cincinnati where he played 13 seasons as a starter for the team with 11 straight pro bowls. He was voted several times as the Offensive Linemen of the Year, and became a member of the 75th anniversary NFL team. Once he retired he was inducted into the NFL Pro Football Hall of Fame. Years later he founded the Anthony Munoz Foundation. A place helping children mentally, physically, and spiritually. He has raised nearly $12 million dollars to impact 25 thousand kids.

Some people think Anthony's Hall of Fame success started with the Bengal's phone call, but that was just a chapter in his journey. His story was full of obstacles and struggles he had to overcome to get him to that phone call. What led him there was the principle his mother gave him: "Move forward. Do your best with what you've got, and never give up."

Our culture loves to tell stories like Anthony's, but our culture doesn't want you to live them. Our culture likes the easy road. Our society spends millions of dollars on quick fix dieting programs so you can lose weight "fast and easy." We hurry to work at jobs where we can make money quickly with little effort.

Let me ask you something, if you were in a conversation amongst your friends and someone described another individual as "easy," what would you think? In my experience I have come to learn that we do not think highly of people when they are called this. Why? Because despite our culture telling us to find shortcuts to get what we want, we know that these remedies will not bring peace to our hearts.

If you are looking for something lasting make the hard decision now that will benefit you in the end. Build habits and foster discipline that become repetitive moments in your story. It is a struggle, but if you can overcome the obstacles, like Anthony Muñoz, you too will become the hero of your story.

"Blessed is the man who endures trial, for when he has stood the test he will receive the crown of life which God has promised to those who love him."
— James 1:12

20. BE VIRTUE

Throughout this book I have challenged you to think about who you are. To reject culture's definition and choose to see who you are by examining your story.

We often succumb to the definitions our culture creates because definitions help our minds to comprehend concepts and ideas more clearly. Thus we define each other. We label each other. We use titles to describe one another. But have you ever thought that there might be a different way to define each other? A better way?

I have explained to you that you are your story, a compilation of the moments, chapters and books of your life. I have presented ways that will help you better craft and tell your story. However, not everyone is going to take the time to listen. People get caught up in their busy lives. With only 24 hours in the day, people have to pick and choose what and who they listen to. So how should we define ourselves? Let's look to the business world.

How do brands define who they are? Businesses spend millions of dollars each year building their brand through marketing and advertising so the company will have brand recognition. The brands depicted are successful at this. You and I can instantly recognize one or more of these brands.

What do you think of when you think of Starbucks? How about Nike? We associate different values with each brand. When I think of Nordstrom I think of the experiences I have had both as a customer and working at the department store as a sales associate. When a woman came to me with ripped jeans she bought two years prior, I smiled and told her, "We don't have this pair of jeans in the store anymore, but why don't you look for another pair. I'll take care of this for you."

As a customer myself I have returned products back to Nordstrom that I didn't believe fit my needs. Every time the sales associates took back the product with no questions asked.

Impeccable service is something Nordstrom values as a company. The company demonstrates this value by ensuring every interaction the customer experiences includes some kind of incredible service. Whether you are dealing with a return, you need assistance to find the right gift, or you need someone to style you for a summer cruise, Nordstrom provides wonderful service to its customers. Nordstrom shows its value of service through the stories they create with their customers.

When we as people explain to others who we are, we look past our personal values and go straight to what we do. Go ahead, jump on Instagram, LinkedIn or Twitter and notice the bios of the people you follow. When I do, I find things like, "CEO," "Author," "Data Analyst," "Reporter," or "Social Media Strategist." I also find some more playful titles like, "Runner," "Lover of lipstick," and even the Olympic ice skater Adam Rippon as "Super-skater." This tells me what you do, but not *who* you are. We define company brands with values, yet we define ourselves with titles. This is a major problem! We are spending hundreds of hours and millions of dollars building company brands, but we have yet to give the same amount of time and attention to our own brand. The brand that we wear throughout our entire lives!

Look back to the timeline you created. Find the recurring themes in your life. What qualities did you demonstrate when you were faced in a time of trial? What about when you were experiencing a season of bliss? What values do you demonstrate consistently?

This process might prompt you to write more moments on your timeline. Go ahead and add them. Maybe you notice you show love, service, or forgiveness often. If so, these are your values which fuel your personal brand. You might recognize that you've been showing more anger than joy. This time of reflection can also be an opportunity for you to intentionally navigate your journey moving forward, to take steps that will positively impact who you will become.

The best brands uphold values, what values are you living your life by?

"Find out who you are and be that person. That's what your soul was put on this earth to be. Find that truth, live that truth and everything else will come."
— Ellen DeGeneres

21. A MOTHER'S STORY

A mother and her eight-year-old son walked in their local grocery store, just how they always had on Thursdays. This Thursday though, the pair ran into an old family friend. It had been many years since they last spent time together.

"My word," the old friend gasped. "Look how big he has gotten!"

The two women chatted for a few moments, catching up on life as old friends do. Then the old friend directed a question to the young boy.

"What do you plan to be when you grow up?"

With no hesitation the young boy answered, "I want to be kind and brave!"

His mother couldn't help but smile. Their family's anthem was to be kind and brave. She had always told her kids that their job wasn't who they were.

"Character, that's who you are," she'd explain to them.

To hear her son answer the question of what he "wants to be" with character and not a career... had her feeling she was doing something right.

Once asked about this philosophy the mother began to explain further.

"You see," she said, "the thing about this shift of thought is that my kids understand their life doesn't magically begin when they 'grow up.' I mean, we are all still waiting for that to happen after all. My kids know that their life is *now*. Childhood is not just a dress rehearsal for adulthood. Nope! It's a beautiful thing, all on its own. Kids, just like you and me, can be who they want to be today. No need to wait.

My son wants to be a person who is kind and brave and the best part is, he is already that! He knows that 'success' isn't dependent on what job he lands. He knows he will be successful if he continues to practice kindness and courage wherever he goes. Currently he is a kind and brave eight-year-old and soon he will be a kind and braver high schooler who will maybe be a kind and brave coach and maybe a kind and brave father or entrepreneur or teacher. His roles will change but his character will always stay the same. My son is already who he wants to be. So now, he can go about being himself forever."

Just like the eight-year-old boy you too can be who you want to be right now. Be yourself then just do the next right thing. Don't wait. Life starts right now. It's as simple or as complicated as that.

-An adapted story from Glennon Melton

22. TELL YOUR STORY

There I was, training for my second marathon. This time I was dreaming of qualifying for the Boston Marathon. I told my friends of my plans. Often they would check in with me to see how the progress of my training was going. When I would casually chat with other runners, I would ask them for their advice, especially those who had achieved my goal. This allowed me to gain wisdom from those who had been before me and, more often than not, people were eager to share their training tips.

One morning I was teaching a spin class. It was at a new gym I had not worked at before. Unfamiliar with the people in the room I introduced myself before beginning the class. As I was warming up the class, two more ladies popped in. "Sorry we are late," one of the women said, "We got back later than expected from a race in Oklahoma."

Both women were sporting finisher race t-shirts. I asked about the race. Eagerly, they both shared their day old memories.

"It was a beautiful day. Great race."

"Thirty-two down, eighteen to go."

I learned that together they were working towards running a marathon in every state of the country before celebrating their 60th birthday. As it turned out the two ladies were twins.

I was about one month from the marathon I was training for, and a little nervous. The week prior, a running friend asked about my goal of qualifying for the Boston marathon and about my running history. He told me not to get bummed if I didn't achieve it. "That's a lofty goal," he said. He wanted to provide me with a realistic perspective. However, I was dissatisfied by his words. I shared this along with my aspirations, with the two women as we continued our conversation.

"That's hodge-podge! Don't listen to him," said the first twin.

"You are going to do this! What kind of shoes do you have? You need a new pair for the race. You should be breaking them in right now," the second twin followed up.

Conventional running wisdom would tell you to buy a pair of running shoes every five hundred miles. When training for a marathon that means a runner should get new shoes about every three months. I had bought a new pair of running shoes when I started training in the spring. My budget was tight. I was working a lot of different odd jobs, and my income wasn't steady as I was still trying to figure out life and work post my TV news days. I shared with the twins that I wasn't planning to buy a new pair of shoes.

"Your running shoes are like your tires. You have to have good tires for the race," one of the twins encouraged me.

I shared with them more about my situation, how I had recently quit my job and was working doing my own freelance work. They were smiley and hopeful. I finished teaching the spin class and everyone seemed to be in a good mood.

"I need to go run to my car to grab something. Don't go anywhere. I will be right back," one of the women said.

When she returned, she walked right up to me and grabbed my hand.

"I want you to have this," she said, looking into my eyes.

There, in my hand she placed a fifty-dollar bill.

"Use this to help you buy your tires. You need good tires," she explained.

I resisted at first. Was I worthy of this generosity? Regardless of my thoughts and my initial hesitation the twin persisted.

A week later I was running the streets with a new set of kicks. On the back of each shoe was a heart with their initials scribbled on them. A reminder of two more people who believed in me and my story.

It can be uncomfortable to share with someone what's on your heart, especially to a total stranger. You have to be willing to be vulnerable. By sharing your story, the struggles and the victories you are facing, God will show his love to you in incredible ways. Are you ready to see God's radical love for you?

"And my God will supply every need of yours according to his riches in glory in Christ Jesus."
– Philippians 4:19

23. A BROKEN STORY

In a small room more than a dozen Air Force officers sat in a line, ready to serve justice in a court martial trial. One of the instructor pilots was accused of sexually assaulting different groups of girls at a nearby college campus. This type of behavior can lead to strict punishment in our regular court system. For someone wearing our nation's uniform, the repercussions are even more severe as they are held to higher standards.

To defend the Air Force instructor, his lawyer brought in different people from the base to attest to his character. One pilot student got on the stand and shared how the instructor modeled respect and care for others. You could see the admiration in her eyes as she spoke about her instructor. She explained how he and his wife often hosted people at their home while others went off drinking. The girl explained how this provided her with a place to socialize, without the pressure of alcohol.

The young girl was impressed by his work, and how he went above and beyond for her and his other students. She then told a story that brought her to tears. It was when her husband was serving in the Middle East. She recalled the day when he went missing and she believed her husband had been killed. Panicked, racing around the base searching for answers, the instructor pilot stayed by her side the entire time. He got her the things she needed, when she needed them. As she told the story, you could see just how much his compassion meant to her during this time.

Afterwards, the college girls, who accused the pilot of his

sexual behaviors, individually took the stand. Each of them described the experience they had while sitting in the student center. As they told their story, they went through the instructor pilot's actions moment by moment as he engaged in the inappropriate behaviors. They shared pictures of the event they had captured on their phones.

It sounded as if the two parties in the courtroom had described two different people. One was a compassionate, ethical and moral man. The other was one consumed by his sexual desires. The evidence from the young college girls was strong, too strong for the instructor pilot's student's story to prove his innocence for his alleged sexual assaults. The jury found the instructor pilot guilty.

Then both lawyers brought their witnesses back to the stand to influence the jury's decision for the instructor pilot's punishment. The defense attorney summoned the instructor pilot's student.

Once she got back on the stand the girl was informed the instructor pilot had been found guilty. Tears began to fall down her face. She looked as if she had been thrust into chaos as she tried to puzzle together how the same man who was there comforting her during one of the scariest moments of her life could be the same man who sexually assaulted young girls on a college campus.

You can write any story you want; a story of virtue, love, and giving, but if you don't live out the story in every facet of your life, it will merely become a fantasy. The instructor pilot lived out his story in only pockets of his life. If you want a story that reads the same to everyone, you must live that story to every audience you have.

"He who is faithful in a very little is faithful also in much; and he who is dishonest in a very little is dishonest also in much."
— Luke 16:10

24. LIVE YOUR STORY

Growing up, one of my mother's favorite phrases was "Actions speak louder than words." This phrase helped me to navigate truth. When I watched the actions of others I found myself better able to answer the question, "Who are you," without asking the question directly. As Ghandi said, "My life is my message."

In John 15:5 it reads "I am the vine, you are the branches. He who abides in me, and I in him, he it is that bears much fruit, for apart from me you can do nothing."

When you first look at a tree, where do you look? I can't help but to look at the colorful leaves in the fall and the blossoming flowers in the spring. Curiosity of the beauty then leads me to a deeper inspection, so I find myself following the branches to the base of the tree.

It's our natural instinct to look at what is in front of us. Actions - the way you carry yourself, what you do, how you speak - are the first characteristics people notice about you. Ninety percent of communication is nonverbal. The actions you take in your story are like the branches John writes about in his gospel. What do your branches say about you? Are your branches blossoming or are they withering away?

God promises, if you let Him be the roots of your life it will bear much fruit. God actually designed us this way. He craves for you and I to live stories that are full of wonder and awe. Do you know someone who lives their life like this? Someone who is joyful, kind, loving, patient and generous in all that they do? Their actions are evidence of their deep relationship with God and understanding of who they are. These types of people also live with personal freedom. It's a hard concept to grasp because when you think about freedom you are naturally inclined to think that it means people do what they want, when they want. However, when a person has personal freedom it actually means that they have an understanding of what matters most and what matters least.

Every day we have to make thousands of decisions. Some decisions might seem unimportant like what do I drink with my breakfast while other decisions feel more monumental in our lives like, what college will I attend. No matter what question we are facing, the decision we make will allow us to do one of two things; it will either make us move closer to who we are meant to become or further away. People who have personal freedom are able to quickly answer the questions that come their way because they know who they are and thus, what they value. They have clarity in their life to be able to say 'no' to what's not important which gives them the ability to say a more meaningful 'yes' to the things that matter the most.

To have personal freedom is not easy, just like it's not easy to follow Jesus. As Jesus said, "If any man would come after me, let him deny himself and take up his cross and follow me" (Matthew 16:24). Though followers of Jesus are clear on their values it means sometimes they have to make decisions that are not popular by society. Our culture tells us to be selfish, when God tells us to deny ourselves. Followers of Christ choose justice and serve those who are less fortunate rather than spending their time building their own palace for personal pleasure. He guides them with encouragement and inspiration along their life's journey.

"Through discipline comes freedom."
— Aristotle

25. I DARE YOU

When is the last time you sat down with someone and openly shared your story? How did you feel when you did? Were you nervous or scared to walk people down the path that you have journeyed?

As human beings we all crave to love and be loved. To be loved we must build intimacy by opening our hearts and sharing our true selves. This takes an incredible amount of vulnerability, a willingness to share despite the possibility of rejection from others. More often, we let our fear win and choose to mask ourselves. This way, if we do experience rejection we don't have to feel the pain from it because we are protected by the masks we have put on to cover our true selves. It's a great way to shield yourself from all the hurt you experience. However, that shield also acts as a barrier preventing you from connecting authentically with those around you.

I remember the day I learned to just go for it. It was during a high school cheer practice. We were working on our back handsprings. A few of us all had the right technique. The one thing we lacked was the confidence to try it without a spotter. As I stood by a friend getting ready for her turn I blurted out, "Don't think. Just do. Just do it!"

She looked at me and smiled. "Just do it," she repeated back to me.

We were equipped with the right mechanics. It was our heads getting in the way - telling us we couldn't. As soon as we stopped thinking so much we were able to perform our back handsprings effortlessly.

The beauty of your story is that it's yours. No one can discount the feelings and resolutions that come from it. I encourage you too, just do it— share the journey that has made you who you are. That is, after all, what we want to answer, right? "Who am I?"

If ever any doubt, take comfort in who God says you are. You are wondrously made for good works (Psalms 139:14). He plans for welfare for you, to give you a future and a hope. (Jeremiah 29: 11)

Now, I dare you. Share your story. The people I've met who do, live more passionately, love more deeply and experience their journey with more zest. Why? Because they do not let fear paralyze them. These people embrace all the feelings of life. Do they experience pain and rejection? Yes. Not all people are going to connect with you and your story. But, when these people connect with others who do appreciate their story, they are rewarded greatly with a feeling of love that only true intimacy can create.

"Have I not commanded you? Be strong and of good courage; be not frightened, neither be dismayed; for the Lord your God is with you wherever you go."
— Joshua 1:9

ABOUT THE AUTHOR

Lindsey answers the question, Who am I; with three words. Uplift. Enlighten. Encourage. She uplifts by telling compelling stories, enlightens by sharing thought provoking ideas and concepts and encourages people to be their best self. She's often called an inspirational cheerleader. She'd tell you she got great practice during her high school years.

Her passion for story led her to a career in broadcast. Lindsey worked in Texas and Ohio as a TV news reporter before discovering how the story writing process can help people and organizations uncover their true purpose.

Today, Lindsey works as an Organizational Effectiveness Consultant in Portland, Oregon. She facilitates leadership courses and coaches companies how to embrace what she believes are their best assets, people.

Lindsey loves making new friends. Say hello!

Instagram @lindsey_wopschall   **Twitter** @wopschall

Made in the USA
Middletown, DE
07 July 2018